Why Don't You Just Send Me Back?

Adoption: A Story of Expectation, Truth and Compassion

I0141383

Why Don't You Just Send Me Back?

Adoption: A Story of Expectation, Truth and Compassion

Becky Walker

YouSpeakIt

PUBLISHING

*The Easy Way
to Get Your Book
Done Right*™

www.YouSpeakItPublishing.com

ISBN: 978-1-945446-40-5

This book is dedicated to my wonderful daughter Emilia.

I loved you yesterday, I love you today,
and I will love you tomorrow.

Acknowledgments

Bringing a book to life is not a solitary process. I am immensely grateful to the following persons for their support, advice, and encouragement:

Keith and Maura Leon, Cameron, Nida, and the other staff of YouSpeakIt Publishing for making this as easy as possible through your calmness and for the reminders to breathe, trust the process, and speak from my heart.

Chris Collins, at American Design Company, for the book cover design, title suggestion, and wise counsel.

Bill Stierle, at Corporate Culture Development, for his enthusiastic—*Yes!*—when I first asked if he thought it would be possible to apply certain information to adoptive parent/child relationships.

Bob Lott, for loving and cheering me on every step of the way.

Sherrie McCaskill for being my business partner, encourager—that covers so much—and best friend in the world!

Most importantly, my daughter Emilia, for accepting me as her mother, despite my flaws.

Contents

Introduction

Why Don't You Just Send Me Back? is a book about the ultimate, bothersome question that often lurks in the mind of an adopted child.

Can I send this child back? is the variation of that question that haunts the minds of many adoptive parents.

This book is about understanding the realities of the beliefs of many adopted children who have experienced early childhood trauma. It discusses how these beliefs show up in their troublesome behaviors even when they are living in a safe and encouraging environment where they can feel happy and thrive.

This book is intended to help ensure that adoptive parents do not fall into the trap of negative thinking, such as:

- *We are failures.*
- *We don't know how to parent.*
- *There's nothing we can ever do to form a connected relationship with our adopted child.*

This book will help provide you clarity about what's really going on, so you can focus your thoughts and efforts on the actions that can give you the relationship you want.

I wrote *Why Don't You Just Send Me Back?* to tell you about the adoption journey my daughter and I have been on. Through our story, I want to help other adoptive parents know that the things they experience and feel are not unique to them. I understand how you feel. I understand what you are going through. I understand how difficult it can be every day as you try to bring a sense of connectedness to your relationship with your adopted child.

I wrote this book so that you would know that you are not alone, and that there's someone who knows the things adopted children do can be subtle and painful. Just because these actions are not seen by other family members, friends, or acquaintances does not mean they don't take place. I want you to know that I know how you feel.

I encourage you to write notes in this book. Have a pen or pencil handy and mark the parts of the story that resonate with you. I've presented the information in a way that I think is a logical progression, but some information may not become clear until later in the book. So, I encourage you to go back and forth. Please feel free to contact me or the support staff at Beyond Adoptions if you have questions. I would like the opportunity to speak with you, hear your story, and answer your questions.

I hope that reading this book provides you with clarity. I hope it provides *Aha! moments* where you recognize elements of my story or examples that are similar to what you've experienced in your own journey with your adopted child. I hope this book changes the way you see your adopted child.

And, I hope this book makes it clear that you are the right parent for your child, and that you and your child can have the connected relationship you desire.

CHAPTER ONE

My Journey With My Adopted Daughter

THE BEGINNING OF THE RELATIONSHIP

The beginning of the relationship between my daughter and me was full of expectation and optimism. I believed that God would connect me with the right child. My heart was open and eager at the prospect of providing the loving and nurturing family she needed. There were challenges early on, but I came to understand more about her, and she turned out, of course, to be the right girl; the one who I believe God provided.

The Idea to Adopt and the Application

My story began when I was sitting in a Sunday morning church service in early 2005. I had what I call a *knowing moment*. Maybe you've had moments like this, in which something is born inside of you. It's born in the place inside of you where you believe you understand something very clearly for the first time, where the idea takes form. My knowing moment was that there was a child that I was supposed to adopt. Although I had two stepsons in a previous marriage, I did not have any children of my own at the time.

After the church service, I came home and immediately started an internet search to educate myself about adoption requirements. I told my husband that I felt we were supposed to adopt. When he said he was willing, we began our journey. We were fortunate to live near The Gladney Center for Adoption, a well-known adoption center in Fort Worth, Texas, that has been in operation for over a hundred years.

We submitted our application to adopt two girls, age four or older, with a preference for sisters from the Ukraine. We wanted this combination because we felt that we needed school-aged children due to our full-time work schedules. We wanted siblings so that one child would not be lonely. And, while having a boy would have been wonderful, I had a sense that we were to have a daughter. Since we were interested in older children, we were invited by the Gladney Center to participate in their Bright Futures Program. We agreed. Our journey was underway.

Our Time Together Before the Adoption Was Finalized

During the application process, I refused to look at videos or photographs of prospective adoptees. Although this is a common way of identifying a child for potential adoption, I firmly believed that God would provide the children we were supposed to adopt. Because I had requested to adopt sisters, I was surprised in July 2005 to receive an email from the adoption agency providing pictures of only one five-year-old girl.

Later that summer, we met the girl who would become our daughter. Her name was Emiliya Nikolayevna Gridina. She stayed with us in our home for more than two weeks. She was bright, energetic, healthy, independent, funny, and charming. At the end of the visit, we had to send her back to Russia with the other kids who had come for the Bright Futures Camp.

We made two trips to Russia to begin the formal process of meeting the review requirements and going to court to finalize the adoption. The first trip was in October of 2005, and the second in February of 2006. On February 20, 2006, we stood in the Russian court and were granted the approval to adopt Emiliya as our daughter. We decided to keep her beautiful name, but Americanized the spelling slightly to Emilia.

Our time with her in our home and in Russia was very positive. She was determined to let the other kids in the orphanage know that we were the parents to take *her* home and that we didn't belong to anybody else. It reinforced my belief that she was as happy as we were that we were going to be a family. Then, on March 6, 2006, we brought her home to the United States.

Bringing Her Home

After the adoption was final in the Russian court, we arrived at the orphanage late at night to pick her up and take her with us. We brought a live plant to the orphanage because the tradition was to trade a live plant, a living thing, for the living person being taken away from the orphanage. I had to strip her naked because she couldn't take anything from the orphanage, and I dressed her in new clothes. She said goodbye to the orphanage workers and the eleven or so boys and girls of her age with whom she had lived. We went out to the car to make the four-hour drive to Moscow.

As we got into the car, it was very, very cold. There was deep snow all around, and the car was not warmed up. So, when we got in the car I instinctively reached out and pulled her to me to keep her warm. This is when everything changed. She forcefully pushed me away and refused to let me hold her. I remember that moment distinctly because it was the first of many painful moments that I would experience in the following days, weeks, months, and years. It quickly became clear that she didn't want anything to do with me.

Other than allowing me to bathe her, wash and dry her hair, and provide her with food, she did not want to associate with or be touched by me. She did not want to speak to me. I could not tuck her in bed or kiss her goodnight. She refused to be near me. In contrast, she was much more okay with being near my husband. That was a good thing because it helped us get her home and get her settled. But, it was very clear while we were still in Russia that the connection and happiness we had thought would come automatically wasn't even close to showing up. We were not prepared for that.

THE AWFUL MIDDLE TIME

I am sharing this time with you because I have found again and again that it resonates with many adoptive parents who have opened their lives and homes and hearts to an adoptive child, and then been surprised by the reality with which they have been faced. I share this so I can make it clear that I understand what many other adoptive parents have experienced. I can't remember a time in my life when I felt like such a failure. I went into a period of denial as I grieved my disappointment. I experienced depression because this truly felt like the darkest time in my life.

Her Disruptive Behaviors

When we arrived home in the United States, we were extremely fortunate to have access to a young woman, Alison, who was fluent in Russian. We found her through a family connection, and she lived with us for the first three months after we brought Emilia home. She was a young American woman who had worked with Doctors Without Borders in Russian orphanages. She was an absolute miracle!

As Alison conversed in Russian with Emilia, it became clear that our new daughter was completely uninterested in my husband and me as parents.

The statement that really stuck with me was, "She has complete disdain for you."

We were informed that Emilia didn't care if we were there or not. She didn't want to be our daughter. She didn't feel like this was home. We were immaterial to her. As you can imagine, this was a huge blow to us. She would tolerate my husband's presence and adopted a very manipulative pattern of interacting with him. Meanwhile, I could not travel alone with her in a car because she would try to jump out.

Emilia would not stay in a room with me alone. She would try to run away. She kicked and bit me. She would hide out of the peripheral vision of other people and *flip the bird* at me. This began a very difficult time. My world—where I had almost always gotten along easily with family, friends, classmates, colleagues, nieces, nephews, and my own stepsons—was now turned upside down. Nothing I tried seemed to work, including what had worked for me in the past with other children. Nothing worked with this child who was determined to show her anger and push me away at every turn.

My Pain

It is hard to describe how painful it was for me to realize what I thought would be a relatively easy relationship—requiring only love, attention, safety, and nurturing—wasn't going to be. I sought help from my adoption agency. I turned to my minister, a local child study clinic, and our pediatrician. I turned to friends and other parents. I tried to find something—anything—that would help me to understand why this child was so angry, and why she didn't want to have anything to do with me. I was stunned that a young child who needed so much seemed determined to reject my efforts to provide her with family and love.

A Story

When Emilia came to live with us, she really wanted to swim, an activity she had not had the opportunity to do before. I introduced the idea by drawing a picture of someone swimming:

My best attempt at a stick figure in a swimming pool. I was not an art major—or minor!

With a lot of gesturing and pointing at the picture (I did not speak Russian, and she did not yet speak English), I communicated the invitation. She eagerly smiled, nodded her head vigorously and gestured with a *thumbs up!* I then turned the picture over and showed her a different picture:

Emphasis on the seatbelts!

This picture was to address the fact that to this point, we had not been able to go anywhere in a car together without her trying to jump out of the moving car. I pointed at the smaller figure and the seat belt. I gestured.

"Seatbelt, swim!" followed by, "No seatbelt, no swim!"

I checked for understanding and she vigorously nodded in agreement.

This established a routine of going to a local YMCA pool together. She loved being in the water. I loved that I was able to touch and hold her as she happily relied on me to keep her afloat. We laughed and played our way through many visits to the pool. I cried with happiness the day she gathered up her courage and dared to jump from the edge into my waiting arms.

We had a routine in which we got a fun snack each time before we headed back to the car to return home. Staying in her car seat and keeping her seat belt latched was never an issue. She never once tried to jump out of the car.

Yet, when we re-entered our house, she immediately reverted to her previous demeanor. More than once, she kicked me in the shin and ran off to her room, and I returned to my puzzled state and waited for the next opportunity for the pure joy of seeing her happy, relaxed, and enjoying simply being a kid.

Emilia's rejection was a huge puzzle. And, it was made more difficult because my husband and I were not on the same page. While she was dismissive and did not want to be with me, she was manipulative with him, and would do things to me and then turn to do the opposite to him. Under this new pressure, he and I began to struggle with our own relationship. We were experiencing and perceiving her behaviors differently. Rather than pulling together, we drifted further and further apart. Finally, my husband and I divorced.

Her Dark Thoughts Surface

The difficulties in my relationship with my daughter lasted for a long time. They got better year by year, but only incrementally. We found a way to live together and interact that was mostly peaceful, or at least peaceful on the surface. I attended her school events, drama, dance and vocal performances. I took her to swim lessons. I threw birthday parties and we attended traditional extended family events. We decorated Christmas trees and got ornaments to commemorate the key events or things she liked best each year. We started an annual ritual of buying gifts for two Salvation Army Angel Tree recipients. But we were certainly not connected. We didn't share closeness or warmth. She still was rigid and unyielding when I would hug her.

From the beginning, she would go to other adults, even complete strangers, and let them wrap their arms around her. They would say things to me like:

- *I don't understand what your problem is because she's just great with us.*

- *She is always so polite and courteous. I wish my child acted just like her.*

- *She is so beautiful, and loving, and giving.*

The truth is, I knew *all* these things about Emilia. I had recognized her kind and empathetic nature from the very beginning at the orphanage. I watched her engage easily with other adults in conversation as early as the age of seven. I was often filled with pride and amazement at her politeness and enthusiasm for helping others out in public.

And, I also knew that she struggled with being part of a group, team, or class. She longed for and tried to have friendships with peers. I was aware as she failed to establish anything more than fleeting friendships with classmates and kids at summer camps. I heard her report repeatedly, often tearfully, that she was *always* nice and they were *always* mean. When she pushed back against authority in school after school, I was summoned to numerous meetings with teachers, principals, and school counselors to discuss her rudeness to adults, disruptiveness in class, and attacks on other kids. I established plans with those same principals, teachers, and school counselors for how to help her get through difficult moments inside the classroom.

She saw counselors and therapists and took medications intended to hold her back from the brink of anger and give her time to process thoughts and feelings. We found her first written report of a desire to kill herself when she was nine years old.

Inside of our home, and even subtly when we were around other people, my daughter would flinch at my touch and would never actually hug me. This tenuous way of interacting continued until seven years after her adoption, when she wrote some information that I came across. In it she had laid out the fact that she didn't like me being her mother. She didn't like me at all.

She wrote that she wished that, if she got a chance, *she could put a kitchen knife in my back.*

I couldn't believe what I was reading.

I asked her, "Is this true?"

With an emotionless look, she said to me, "I would rather have anyone else in the world than you as my mother."

Even as I recall those words today, my eyes fill with tears. It was the hardest thing I had ever been told. My heart sank to its lowest point.

REACHING A CONNECTED RELATIONSHIP

Despite the hard beginning and the awful middle time, our adoption story today is very happy.

Difficulties in having a connected relationship with a child is by no means exclusive to adoptive families. Having a truly connected relationship with any child takes attention and determination. It *is* possible to move from disconnection to connection. I have done it. Other parents have done it. You can do it, too!

Something Had to Change

After I faced the dark reality that something was seriously wrong, I recognized that, as the adult and parent, it was *my* responsibility to create change if I wanted our relationship to improve. I knew that I had to begin with an examination of myself because, as we all know, the only thing we can truly control is ourselves and our actions. I determined that I would review the things that I had been doing as a parent, and I started down a path of exploration. I committed to myself to be brutally honest no matter how uncomfortable it might make me.

I examined my own past, parenting, and relationships—what had worked for me, and especially what had not worked for me. It required me to face some facts about myself, and that didn't always come easily. It required me to decide what I wanted the outcome to be and to find the path of how to get there. I accepted the uncomfortable truth that I needed to change before I could expect anything about the relationship with my daughter to change. This was not easy for me, but I knew I had to do it. I felt like my daughter's life depended on it.

The Re-Education of Becky

The change-path that I have been on has been truly amazing. Every little change and every little realization that I have come to has led to the next thing that I needed to realize or change. When I look back down this path, I can see how people, information, and circumstances came into my life at just the right time. Each of these helped to move me from where I was to the place that I wanted to be.

A pivotal moment in my journey of relationship-healing occurred the first time I heard my friend, Bill Stierle, of Corporate Culture Development, say the following: "All human behaviors are clues to met and unmet needs."

We will explore this idea more in Chapter Four.

The next major aspect of my re-education had to do with my communication skills, or, actually, my lack of some particular communication skills.

I was introduced to two significant ideas:

- Thinking Preferences
- Compassionate Communication

The first idea, *Thinking Preferences*, means that all people have preferred styles of thinking through which they filter their interactions with others and the world.

Compassionate Communication is an alternative name for *Nonviolent Communication* (NVC), created by Marshall Rosenberg in the 1960s. Mary Mackenzie uses initial capitals in referring to Compassionate Communication in her book, *Peaceful Living: Daily Meditations for Living with*

Love, Healing, and Compassion. I prefer to use the alternate terminology, Compassionate Communication.

I have become convinced if we change only one thing in our interactions with our adopted children, it should be to practice Compassionate Communication. When we do, those interactions improve. And, if we *teach our children* to use Compassionate Communication, the relationship itself will become more connected.

Seeing My Daughter with New Eyes and a New Heart

I am grateful for the experiences that I have had even though they were far from easy for my daughter and me. Now, I am fully aware that she did not set out to be difficult. I no longer think of her as having done things to me. I came to the realization that she has always done the best she could with what she had to work with, and I've done the same. And now, I recognize that, while I was certainly eager and willing to be her parent, I was completely unprepared and ill-equipped.

I tried to find resources to help me, but I could not find them early on. Now, because of the self-education I've done, I have been able to reach a point where I see my daughter through new eyes and with a renewed heart. I can see that her disruptive behaviors and apparent disdain were rooted in trauma and experiences that had occurred early in her life. Essentially, she had no choice but to do the things that she did.

Once I was able to see her behavior as the representation of her unmet emotional needs, I was at last in a position to change our relationship. I had changed sufficiently so that I could introduce the opportunity—the safe place—for her to let go of old patterns that had given her a false sense of being in control and had, instead, contributed to her ongoing anxiety and isolation. Then, our relationship became connected.

EXPECTATION

Expectation is the heart of hope and sorrow.
~ Dan Trevarthen

CHAPTER TWO

Relationship Expectations of Adoptive Parents and Adopted Children

PARENTING THE WAY WE WERE PARENTED

Often, parents approach their parenting of their own children based on how they themselves were parented. Your perception of how you were parented, positive or negative, informs your own parenting style. It is natural to parent based on your perception of what felt *right* or *wrong* in the parenting you received. But, there are opportunities to examine the way you were parented and to decide if it gets you to the connected relationship you want with your adopted children.

Parenting Patterns and Strategies: The Fifties and Sixties

Like most things, parenting patterns have gone through an evolution over the years.

In the United States in the 1950s and '60s—this was the time I was a child—popular parenting strategies could be described with the word: *discipline.*

Popular ideas included:

- Children should speak only when spoken to.
- Children are to be seen and not heard.
- Children must respect their elders.

I was raised in a conservative environment, and *spare the rod, spoil the child* was a well-known sentiment in parenting while I was growing up.

As a child, these were the familiar guiding principles for me, and pretty much everyone I knew embraced them. These ideas were so universally accepted in my hometown in Arkansas, that, in our neighborhood, one mother was free to discipline and even punish another woman's child and vice versa. And, when you got home, your own parent would often administer additional punishment *for good measure.*

Parenting Patterns and Strategies: The Seventies Through Nineties

During the time of the disco craze, parenting children moved into a phase of *love.*

As we moved through the 1970s, '80s, and '90s, the sentiment became: *Love is enough!*

This was the time of flower children, hippies, and then yuppies. One might hear parents talk about their child being their best friend. Parents during that time wanted to provide their kids with the material goods and opportunities they never had. They didn't want to treat their children the way that they had been treated.

There was an idea that statements should always be positive and parents should avoid saying anything negative to their child. *Don't say no!* Don't deny a child what they want. Rather, it was all about positive reinforcement. An example of this was when children were on teams, it became standard to make sure everyone got a trophy. Everyone got a prize. No one was a loser: *It's all about me. I am number one. You are number one. We all are number one.*

Parenting Patterns and Strategies Now

Those old ways of approaching parenting worked to some extent in their own time and place. But, we want to parent our children—to develop a relationship and interact with them—from a place of compassion. We want to create mutual consideration between the parent and child. This is far different than having our young child as our best friend. That is not an appropriate role for a child. They are not equipped emotionally nor experientially enough to assume this role for an adult.

We want to instill values, such as:

- Emotional safety
- Mutual respect
- Healthy choice
- Trust
- Connection

We want to develop a habit of checking in because the message we think we have sent is often not the message the child has received; it is not what they hear. We want to apply parenting strategies in the language of kindness, compassion, and empathy. Most of our parents did not know how to do this for us. It is important to instill these qualities in our everyday interactions with our children so they become self-directed, self-regulated, and grow into age-appropriate, emotionally mature, independent adults.

PARENTS AND CHILDREN BELIEVE A FAIRY TALE

The subject of beliefs is very important because our beliefs impact our understanding about ourselves, our children, and the meanings in our interactions. The beliefs that we have when we are in the process of establishing a new connection through adoption are understandable. We have great expectations. We have hopes and beliefs about the significance, value, depth, and reality of our love; as well as the opportunities we can give children, who through no fault of their own, are in a position to need our help and love.

Pre-Adoption Beliefs: Adoptive Parents

Like many prospective adoptive parents, I had some strong beliefs when I was going through the process of adopting my daughter. One of those beliefs was that she would be happy when she came into a home where she had a mother and father. I thought that she would automatically feel loved. She would be thankful that she now had her own beautiful, comfortable bedroom and toys and no longer had to live in an orphanage.

I have talked to many prospective parents who say they think their adopted child will thrive because they are in a safe place and are loved. Also, some parents believe that once they bring their child home, their child will not be impacted by the bad things that have happened in their past. They believe that the act of giving a child a home that is safe, secure, stable, loving, nurturing, and happy is going to automatically cause their adopted child to be happy, feel loved, and enable them to demonstrate love and gratitude in return.

Pre-Adoption Beliefs: Adopted Child

Adopted children also come into the adoption situation with their own set of beliefs based on their own experiences and expectations. Sometimes, they believe that when they are assigned to a family, they are automatically going to be happy. Sometimes, when they come from an orphanage, and they have never experienced nuclear family life before; they have an idea that life is always going to be fun. They may imagine that there is a big pile of candy they can access all the time, that they will be allowed to do whatever they want to do whenever they want to do it, and they are going to be very happy.

The same beliefs may exist within children who are not from orphanages but have never lived in a stable, safe, or nurturing environment. They may also believe that the act of getting a family, or parents, is going to change their existence into the world they want it to be.

Pre-Adoption Beliefs: Family and Friends

When we adopt a child, their new family extends beyond us. There are usually grandparents, aunts, uncles, cousins, and friends. Extended family and friends often have beliefs much like our own beliefs as adoptive parents. Like us, they believe they have something that is wonderful to provide to a child who needs it.

Many in our extended family will believe our adopted child is so lucky to have been saved from the place where they were, and that our child is going to be so happy in their new environment.

We often hear friends and family members say things like:

- *We can hardly wait for this precious child to get here because she is the luckiest kid on the face of the Earth—she just doesn't know it yet!*

- *He is going to love us and be so happy.*

- *She is going to thrive!*

- *He is going to recognize just how lucky he is.*

I know many adoption stories where the fairy tale seems to have come true. I am grateful that is the reality for those adoptive families. I am grateful for whatever the circumstances were before and after the adoption that allowed bonding, attachment, and connection to occur; for whatever the innate resilience and adaptability was in those adopted children; for the loving and nurturing characteristics of those adoptive parents that were able to connect with the heart-strings of their precious adopted children.

I wish all adoption stories could vibrate from the beginning with the fulfillment of those happy beliefs that time, attention, and love is enough for success.

Actually, I *do* believe that time and attention and love *are* enough, it's just that the amount of time, and the specific demands and characteristics of that love and attention, are not the same in any two adoption stories.

LETTING GO OF EXPECTATIONS

Because of the beliefs we may have about how life is going to be inside our family, it can be shocking when the positive things we believed would exist—the relationships we hoped for—do not automatically materialize. It is easy to create lots of reasons in our minds for why our relationship is not the way we thought it would be. When and if we find ourselves in this circumstance, one of the most freeing moments can be when we let go of the expectations that we had going in, and instead, embrace the truth about the new relationship that has been created.

Everyone—adoptive parents, adopted children, and our friends and family—has expectations about what the new relationship created through adoption is going to be like. Some of those expectations are going to be realized. And sometimes, there will be disappointment and sadness when it becomes clear that other expectations are not going to be fulfilled. But, there is a way to move forward, and as adoptive parents that's where we want to be—moving forward to the connected relationship that we want with our child.

Facing a New Truth

It was difficult for me when I brought my daughter home from Russia and very quickly came to the realization that she was not happy. We learned that she had disdain for us, that she didn't want to be with us, and that we were a disappointment to her. This was shocking, disappointing, and disillusioning; and it took a while for me to come to a place where I could face this new truth. I know that I am not alone in this experience.

There are many adoptive parents who know the unhappy reality of having to accept that what they thought was going to be a very happy, loving, and accepting situation is not going to automatically be any of those things. Of course, no relationship is automatically perfect. But, it can be shocking when the reality and truth is that the difficulties are far beyond what would be considered normal in a relationship.

Mourning the Loss

As an adoptive parent, you may find yourself in a situation in which the reality is not the expected fairy tale. It is normal to go through a time of mourning the loss of what you thought the relationship would be. Humans have a capacity to grieve and feel disappointment, and the emotions that accompany those feelings. You need to do this in a safe place and in a safe way. As parents, we need to allow ourselves to go through this process.

To help you during this time, I highly recommend that you seek a person who knows you and your situation, someone you can trust to hold space for you, such as a:

- Friend
- Coach
- Counselor
- Therapist
- Clergy
- Family member

You will need a person who will allow you to go through the mourning process honestly. I encourage you to give yourself a break and allow yourself to acknowledge your disappointment and your pain and sorrow. It can be hard to do. It's okay. It's necessary. And, it will clear the space in your heart that you need to move forward. Recognize that your needs for connection, love, clarity, and acceptance haven't been met. Your trusted person can also help by providing empathy. Empathy, and in particular self-empathy, is necessary to prepare yourself to move onto the next phase of the relationship.

There is also a huge need for our adopted children to have the opportunity, freedom, and time to mourn their losses, too. We can make the mistake of only thinking of our adopted child as gaining things—parents, a family, safety, a home, a future, and so on. But, there are significant losses in their lives which they must be given freedom and space to process.

I emphasize this need with parents that I work with because they often have the idea that it helps the kids to always keep everything on a positive note. They are often afraid to have conversations about what the child has lost, who and what they miss. But, it's important for our adopted children to mourn their losses and disappointments, too.

Inviting Acceptance

Once we have given ourselves permission to mourn the loss and face the reality of the new relationship, then we need to invite *acceptance of the situation* the way it really is into our hearts and minds.

This can be done by providing empathy for ourselves and recognizing the feelings that we are having:

- Sadness
- Unfairness
- Frustration
- Anger

In the new relationship with your adopted child, it is helpful to be in a position of self-understanding, self-empathy, and self-kindness as you take steps to move forward. After all, just because you're surprised and disappointed doesn't mean that your goal will have changed. A loving, connected relationship with your adopted child is still the main goal. Your dream has not changed. It's your approach that can be modified.

TRUTH

She had arranged her world so that she would
experience the least amount of pain.

~ Tracy Dunn
Sermon at Broadway Baptist Church,
Fort Worth, Texas
March 2017

CHAPTER THREE

Dealing With Truths About a Relationship With an Adopted Child

WE HAVE BELIEFS THAT ARE NOT TRUE

We've just talked about our expectation about what life will be like once we have our adopted child inside our family. We have additional beliefs that can also be troublesome as the reality of the difficulties in connecting with our adopted child become more and more evident. We all have beliefs that control a lot of what we think and how we perceive our world. Our beliefs often control the key actions we take. They underlie the coping strategies that we devise, unconsciously, in order to feel in control in our lives.

Beliefs: Adoptive Parents

As adoptive parents, we have beliefs that we may or may not be conscious of that are based on past experiences and the expectations that we have of life. Sometimes, we can be surprised by the events that occur once we have our adopted child in our home. They are surprising because they are not congruent with one or more of these beliefs.

Here are examples of beliefs that can be troublesome:

- Our parents were successful in parenting us, so using those same strategies to parent our own children will work just fine.

- If we simply love this child *enough*, that love will overcome any problems that we may run into, and this child will feel love and reciprocate with love.

- Parenting should be easy for us. We won't have difficulty if we are doing things correctly.

- We are very bonded with our biological child, so the way we parent clearly will work for any child.

- Other than for very, very minor upsets, the relationship with our child will be easy.

Can you see how beliefs such as these may be troublesome to us if the relationship with our adopted child is difficult?

Even more troublesome can be our subconscious core beliefs about ourselves that may reside silently inside of us. Sometimes, the interactions with an adopted child that resists or refuses closeness can trigger insecurities—unmet needs—within us in ways that we may not have experienced before.

Examples of unmet needs:

- Self-worth
- Lovable-ness
- Acceptance
- Appreciation
- Understanding
- Consideration
- Respect

These unmet needs can be triggered by the tragic survival strategies (words and actions) of a child struggling to overcome their trauma. This can also trigger our own insecurities. Our own sometimes-hidden core beliefs can suddenly assert themselves. And, our old strategies for compensating for our unmet needs no longer work for us in the context of this new relationship.

Beliefs: Adopted Children

Your adopted child has core beliefs as well. This may seem like a strange thing to say, especially if your adopted child is days, weeks, or months old. It is not unusual for an adopted child to have core beliefs that are not helpful to them. For instance, an adopted child will often feel like they are not worthy, or not worth loving. This usually stems from their belief that they need to feel ashamed about something or themselves.

This is not a conscious decision on their part.

I was fascinated when I learned that a very small baby, even just a few days old, may resist relaxing into the arms of its adoptive mother because the heartbeat of the birth mother, the only heartbeat and rhythm it has known throughout its entire life, is now absent. The baby's brain notes the familiar heartbeat is no longer there and begins to compensate in order to survive this separation that is not, in nature, normal.

Often, the fact that they did not continue to be with their biological mother is tragically interpreted within them as not being wanted. It is a short leap from *unwanted* to *unworthy and worthless.* If one is unwanted and worthless, a feeling of shame is not far behind.

> *[Shame is] the nervous system collapse we experience when our present behavior or words are outside the window of tolerance of the humans we are dependent on for community.*
>
> ~ Sarah Peyton
> NVC practitioner and author of *Your Resonant Self*
> NVC IIT 2017 Conference, Los Angeles, California

Adopted children also often have a belief that they have no choice. This makes sense. They didn't get to choose to stay with or leave their biological mother. They didn't get to choose if they went into an orphanage, foster care, or another home. It is easy to understand where such a belief would come from.

Adopted children also have beliefs based on their experiences, especially if they are older. When I speak of *older* children, I am referring to four years of age or older. It is not unusual for them to believe that adults can't be trusted or that adults don't and won't protect them. They often think that *they* need to be in control in order to be safe and protected. This belief is especially reinforced if they have suffered physical trauma or neglect. The adults who should have taken care of them have not. Therefore, their experience in the world, and their belief, is that adults will not protect them.

The existence of these beliefs may seem counterintuitive when you are providing a home that is safe, loving, and nurturing to a child. We need to understand their core belief of shame and unworthiness can be so strong that they're convinced if you knew the *truth* about them, you would not provide a home with safety, love, and everything else you offer. In fact, they are convinced if you knew the *truth,* you would not keep them at all.

Core Beliefs Serve a Purpose

Core beliefs serve a very important purpose in our lives because they help to make sense of experiences that we've had. They serve to normalize our relationship with daily life.

Core beliefs help us cope with events that were traumatic or too troubling to understand. Core beliefs give us a way of manifesting control in our world. This is especially important for an adopted child. The problem comes when the core belief is untrue.

In natural circumstances, a primary caregiver responds to a baby's cry and provides care, warmth, feeding, and support in response to those cries. When those caregiver responses don't happen, the baby's brain reaches conclusions or develops beliefs about what it is and isn't going to get when it uses its normal voice, which is crying. When the use of its voice does not result in a nurturing response, the brain will devise coping strategies in order to fill in the gaps for what is not provided by the caretakers.

A classic example of a coping mechanism is the rocking motion seen in children from some Eastern European orphanages. Their rocking back and forth is a self-soothing action.

The coping strategies based on experience become the beliefs of the child. One of the strongest core beliefs that can be very troublesome is the belief that they are shameful. Another way to describe this is being unworthy.

The core belief of shame underlies many actions of our adopted children.

THE IMPACT OF EARLY CHILDHOOD TRAUMA

In most cases, when there's difficulty in establishing a connected relationship with our adopted children, it is highly likely that early childhood trauma has resulted in coping mechanisms that drive the child's behaviors. So, understanding trauma, how it occurs, and what we can do about it, is essential. As adoptive parents, we need to become fully aware in order to be a part of the healing process that is necessary for our adopted child.

It is impossible to convey the utter importance of understanding that adopted children—all adopted children—have experienced some trauma in their lives. Trauma leads to shame, which leads to coping strategies. This sequence negatively impacts the emotional development that is essential for human beings to form resilience.

Signs and Symptoms of Trauma

Once we can understand that trauma can result in coping behaviors, and the forms that those behaviors often take, it can be relatively simple to begin detecting the signs and symptoms of trauma. Some of the signs are subtle, but once you understand that they are there, they are pretty easy to see.

Examples of signs and symptoms of trauma in an adopted child include:

- The child is not affectionate in the way the parent wants to be affectionate; they may not want to hug, kiss, or cuddle.

- The child is indiscriminately affectionate with strangers instead of their parents.

- The child is hypervigilant because their anxiety is so high that they are constantly on alert.

- The child can develop physical problems including frequent tummy aches, headaches, or fatigue.

- The child identifies themself as the victim of the actions of others, with global statements like: *Everyone hates me,* or *No one is nice to me.*

- The child insists that they haven't done anything except try to be friends with people who are mean to them.

There are many other signs and symptoms of trauma. These are just a sampling:

- Low sense of self-worth
- Difficulty concentrating
- Poor relationships with peers at school
- Lack of ability to demonstrate cause-and-effect thinking
- Destructive to themselves, others, or material things

The Impact of Shame

Shame is a very interesting and important outcome of trauma. While a child will not know what they are feeling, the impact of their belief that they are shameful is very strong in their life.

To quote Sarah Peyton again, "Shame is the most unpleasant effect of any emotion on humans."

That is a very powerful statement. Shame is such a controlling factor in the lives of many adopted kids because it feeds their belief that they are unworthy. It is the foundation of many of the strategies that they use in order to try *not* to connect with someone who is providing them with love and care. It can feel *very* confusing to us as adoptive parents, because we know they have tremendous worth and should not have to suffer shame. But our knowing that and their believing it are two very different things.

We must consider shame from the child's point of view, where thoughts such as the following can lurk:

- *I believe that my biological mother did not want me.*
- *How could I be worth so little that my own mother didn't want me?*
- *I must have done something really bad. I must be bad.*

Adoptive parents understand that there are many reasons why a child will be available for adoption, and there are many reasons why a child is separated from their biological mother. We know that many—perhaps most—times, the separation has nothing to do with the biological mother not wanting the child. But, separation occurs, and in the brain, heart, and belief system of that little human being, separation can be—and all too often is—translated into being unwanted. Therefore, the child feels shame. It can be an underlying motivator in the actions of these children.

Unmet Emotional Needs

The impact of separation, other trauma, and shame leads to the brain creating coping mechanisms in order for the child to function and feel safe in light of their beliefs about their world. The unmet emotional needs can often interrupt and delay emotional maturity that is part of normal human development. For instance, if a child from infant to two years does not have a regular, reliable, nurturing experience with a primary caregiver, that child is likely to have missed out on the bonding and the feelings of comfort, love, touch, and acceptance that is normally conveyed to a human being during that period of time.

Positive interactions from primary caregivers are the building blocks that the human brain uses as it lays the foundation for brain architecture. This is what sets us up for developing emotional maturity over the years, particularly between birth and the age of seventeen. And, it is essential for creating the emotional resilience that enables adults to be autonomous and able to cope independently in the world.

Emotional maturity occurs in a fairly predictable pattern during childhood. Each set of emotional building blocks is set on the preceding ones. It is helpful to understand this about your adopted child. If their emotional maturity is delayed, or if their emotional development is interrupted, then you need to go back and take actions to help fill in the gaps and find ways to help your child get those emotional needs met.

To ask your child to demonstrate cooperation, kindness, and affection at the ages of ten to fourteen years seems reasonable, but it is not *if* they have not had the necessary underlying emotional building blocks of love, acceptance, emotional safety, stability, trust, etc. met earlier in their life.

PARENTS AND CHILDREN HAVE TRAGIC STRATEGIES FOR MEETING NEEDS

As adults, we have usually developed various strategies to get our needs met. We've learned these from our parents, other adults, schooling, religion, the media, and our experiences. When we parent a child who has not lived their early life in a nurturing, secure environment, it becomes obvious where their strategies have taken on tragic types of characteristics.

Our own strategies can have some tragic characteristics, too. It is beneficial to understand our own tragic strategies and how we can replace them with strategies that are more helpful, and it is important that we are able to help our children do the same. This can be a difficult area of self-examination for parents. It certainly was for me.

Self-examining your own tragic characteristics may be difficult because you could be firmly attached to your belief in the validity and necessity of your strategies. You need to stay in a place of self-empathy for yourself as a parent. Recognize that up to this point, you've been doing the best you could with what you've had to work with. That's okay.

As we move forward, you'll want to continue to improve your parenting strategies. You'll want to move effectively toward action and interaction with your adopted child that will result in the connected relationship that you desire so much.

Triggers

A trigger is something that happens when your body experiences an emotional reaction to the occurrence of something external to you. We have all been triggered by external events, including words and actions. The experience results in a particular feeling because one or more of our needs was not being met. Triggers can cause reactions that are not what we desire.

An example of a trigger would be reacting in anger when someone cuts in front of you while you are driving in traffic. It may trigger a feeling of fear because your need for safety was suddenly not met. Or, it may trigger a feeling of anger because your need for consideration was not met. Or both!

When you are interacting with your adopted child, a trigger can come in the form of your child's actions or words. Those actions can range from responses that are relatively insignificant, such as the child rolling their eyes, sticking out their tongue, or staring blankly when spoken to; or, your child may give you responses that are truly outrageous, such as shouting words like: *I hate you, you are stupid!* My heart aches for parents who sorrowfully tell me some of the tragic language their child has thrown at them.

Your child might even break something, throw an object, or take any number of other disruptive or destructive actions.

Your ability to remain calm and in control of your reactions can vary greatly when you are triggered. Unfortunately, the actions of your child and the words they might use are their own tragic strategies to cope with what they are feeling. Your responses to those triggers can be your own tragic strategies. Sometimes, we believe these strategies are the way we should respond as a parent. So, let's explore whether that is truly the case.

Tragic Strategies of Adopted Children

What are some tragic strategies that your adopted child may use?

Most tragic strategies will in some way relate to the child's belief that they need to control their world. From past experiences, they may believe they cannot rely on anybody else. Perhaps they believe that they should not trust an adult because of their prior experience of key adults not protecting them, even hurting them.

These tragic strategies can vary and be as simple as:

- Refusing to answer a basic question
- Lying
- Exploding in anger

A strategy they might use to maintain distance between themselves and someone who is offering them love and connection is to say things like, *no!* or to yell, *I hate you!*

Other tragic strategies might be:

- Throw a tantrum and fall on the floor, kick their heels, and scream
- Steal things or hoard food
- Self-mutilation or self-harm: cut, scratch, or otherwise hurt themselves

When you try to help them understand how to do something, they may hurl insults like, *you're the worst mom ever,* or *you're an idiot,* or expletives that are far worse that I won't quote here.

While these may sound like they're just the petulant words or actions of a child that is undisciplined, out-of-control, or just wants to have their own way, they actually are subconscious strategies that allow the children to continue to hold on to their core belief that they are not safe. Ironically, this feels safer to them than relaxing and accepting your care.

Inflicting pain on you is a strategy for demonstrating a child's own feeling of pain. Often, it is their only way of letting you know just how much they feel inside. In Chapter One, I related the story of my daughter's communicating that if she could, she would put a kitchen knife in my back. This triggered a number of feelings and insecurities for me. I wish I could report that I didn't react to her words. But, I did. I was devastated. I convinced myself that I was a failure as a parent; that we would never have a successful relationship. I became depressed.

Today, I have a much-improved ability to manage that type of triggering event in a different way. Today, I know that her tragic words were her best strategy in that moment for expressing her own, internal pain.

Tragic Strategies of Adoptive Parents

The idea that my ways of interacting with my daughter might also be tragic strategies made me feel very uncomfortable at first. To me, they seemed like strategies that absolutely would work, and should work well. I warn you now: some of my old strategies may also be ones that you currently think are sound and appropriate. Therefore, like me, you may at first feel some resistance within yourself to considering them as *tragic strategies.*

So, what are these strategies?

One tragic strategy is the use of rewards and punishments in order to help a child make a decision about how they are going to behave.

How many times have we heard a parent say phrases like: *If you will stop doing what you are doing, then you'll be able to have ice cream later when we get to the store?*

You might be thinking: *Now, wait a second—there's nothing wrong with saying that. It works.*

And you're right. It does work. The problem is the strategies of reward and punishment result in *temporary* compliance. It certainly works in the short term. But, it does not get to the reason for the behavior that the parent was bothered by.

Another tragic strategy is that we fix things for our children. We fix or attempt to fix their problems for them. As adults and as parents, we yearn so greatly to be able to help our children and to make them feel better. But, it is not a great strategy to do that all the time or even most of the time.

Why?

By fixing things for our children, we are not helping them to:

- Learn to self-regulate
- Become self-directed and resilient
- Provide self-empathy and self-soothing in an appropriate way

- Identify their needs and develop the ability and practice of solving problems

Instead, we trap them into an expectation and habit of getting temporary external relief rather than helping them to establish those essential blocks of emotional maturity that are essential as they continue to grow.

Of course, human babies are helpless, and we must help them get their problems solved. But, as children grow and mature emotionally, it is our responsibility to wean them from us always solving their problems so that they can practice and recognize they can do it on their own. This is one of the ways we get them ready to launch from teenagers into adults when the time is right.

It isn't easy to abandon our tragic strategies and try new tactics. It can be especially hard when we are tired or feeling overwhelmed. Sometimes, it just seems more expedient to fix a problem and move on. I agree. I've certainly been a fix-it parent, and I feel okay about that because I could not make every change I needed to make all at once. I needed to start small.

Small changes will build up to larger changes. The point is this: try not to automatically fix things for your child.

Instead, try the following:

- Collaborate with your child.

- Make suggestions that they can choose a solution from.

- Ask them how they would do something if they knew it would turn out okay.

- And here's a hard one: take the chance of letting them fail.

- Be there to support them in their attempt, and avoid the temptation to do it for them.

- Invite them to talk about how they could do it differently on the next attempt.

Every effort you put forth to encourage your child to solve their own problems will make them more self-reliant, more self-directed, and more confident in their own self-worth. It takes time. It takes patience. It is definitely worth the effort.

COMPASSION

Please help me understand my pain.
                                    ~ Adoptees

CHAPTER FOUR

Compassion Is Key to a Connected Relationship

THINKING STYLES

We have come to the best part of the journey. As we discover for real where our adopted child is emotionally, we can use that knowledge to practice *Compassionate Communication* to lead us to the improved connection we desire. An important part of understanding how to communicate with compassion is to know about the natural thinking styles that we and our children have. Those styles have an immediate impact on our ability to communicate effectively with each other.

This is where a major light bulb lit up for me. It felt like an epiphany when I first saw the Herrmann International Whole Brain® Model and its definitions for various *Thinking Preferences*, outlined in *The Whole Brain Business Book*, by Ned Herrmann and Ann Herrmann-Nehdi.

That moment opened a door to insights about my daughter that caused me to say aloud, "Wow! So that's why she does things the way she does them!"

This is important because seeing our children for who they are and providing them with an understanding of who we are is a huge leap forward in establishing a true connection.

What Are the Thinking Styles?

Please refer to Graph One, entitled, "Whole Brain Model: Thinking Processes." This graph is a metaphorical representation of the brain. It is divided in four quadrants and shows some common characteristics of each thinking style. The upper left quadrant represents the *Rational Self,* the lower left is the *Safekeeping Self,* the lower right represents the *Feeling Self,* and the upper right is the *Experimental Self.* We all have natural preferences for how we think. These preferences are the lens through which we see, hear, interpret, and interact with our world.

WHOLE BRAIN® MODEL: THINKING PROCESSES

CEREBRAL MODE

A Rational Self			D Experimental Self
	Analyzes Quantifies Is Logical Is Critical Is Realistic Likes Numbers Knows about Money Knows How Things Work	Infers Imagines Speculates Takes Risks Is Impetuous Breaks Rules Likes Surprises Is Curious / Plays	

LEFT MODE · RIGHT MODE

	Takes Preventative Action Establishes Procedures Gets Things Done Is Reliable Organizes Is Neat Is Timely Plans	Is Sensitive to Others Likes to Teach Touches a Lot Is Supportive Is Expressive Talks a Lot Feels	
B Safekeeping Self			C Feeling Self

The Whole Brain® model and color scheme are copyrighted material of Herrmann Global LLC. ©2017 Herrmann Global LLC. Adapted by Becky Walker with permission.

LIMBIC MODE

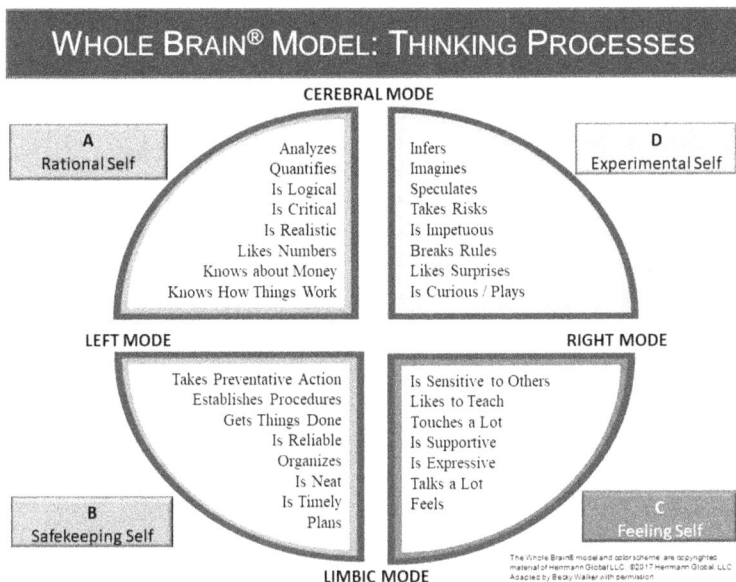

Our four different selves. The Four Selves characterize modes of the whole brain from which we act in response to everyday situation. (N. Herrmann and A. Herrmann-Nehdi, *The Whole Brain Business Book*, second edition, 2015, p. 28. The Whole Brain® model and color scheme, are copyrighted material of Herrmann Global LLC. ©2017 Herrmann Global, LLC. Adapted by Becky Walker with permission.)

Determining Thinking Styles for You and Your Child

Please refer to Graph Two, entitled, "Thinking and Communication Map: Our Four Different Selves," which shows the same brain with some of the types of work professions common to people who have high thinking preferences in each quadrant. It also lists common characteristics of children associated with the various thinking styles.

Find the description of your professional occupation, or what you've always dreamed of doing. And look for characteristics that are descriptive of your child. You may see information in more than one quadrant that describes you, and information in more than one quadrant that describes your child. This makes sense because individuals often have two or three preferred thinking styles. A person can even be multi-dominant and have high preferences in all four quadrants.

THINKING AND COMMUNICATION MAP
OUR FOUR DIFFERENT SELVES

CEREBRAL MODE

A
Rational Self

D
Experimental Self

CHILD	ADULT
Math Whiz	IT Pro
Science	Doctor
Computer Kid	Lawyer
Debater	Banker
Likes Facts	Surveyor
Direct	Pilot/Engineer
Knows how things	Sci. Research
work	Robotics Tech

CHILD	ADULT
Artistic	Artist
Dramatic	Actor
Takes Risks	Inventor
Curious	Architect
Likes Surprises	Entertainer
Breaks Rules	Product Mgr
Creative	Fashion Designer
	Photographer

LEFT MODE   WHOLE BRAIN THINKING   **RIGHT MODE**

CHILD	ADULT
Neat	Organizer
Organizes	Administrative
Dominant in Play	Rule Follower
Perfect Attendance	Accountant
Reads	Operations
Focused	Producer
Notices Details	Police
Controls	

CHILD	ADULT
Musical	Teacher / Coach
Likes PE	Counselor
Expressive	Nurse / Helpers
Reads / Writes	Waiters
Talks a Lot	Cust. Service
Emotional	Sales
Sensitive to Others	
Empathetic	

B
Safekeeping Self

C
Feeling Self

The Whole Brain® model and color scheme are copyrighted material of Herrmann Global LLC. ©2017 Herrmann Global LLC Adapted by Becky Walker with permission

LIMBIC MODE

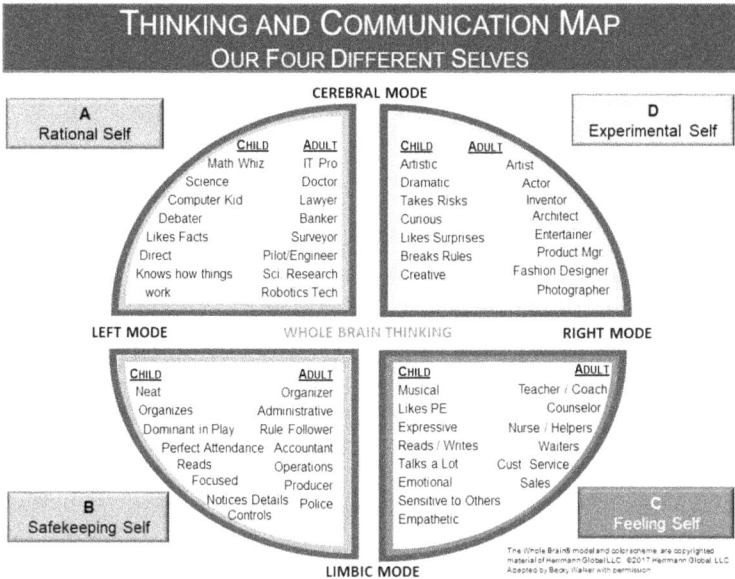

The Four Selves Model provides representative professions of adults and characteristics of children. (The Whole Brain® model and color scheme, are copyrighted material of Herrmann Global LLC. ©2017 Herrmann Global, LLC. Adapted by Becky Walker with permission.)

I have a high preference for three thinking styles: the Feeling Self, the Safekeeping Self, and the Experimental Self. This shows up in my life as I care about the well-being of others and about my relationships (the Feeling Self). I prefer a lot of order and neatness in my world (the Safekeeping Self), and my Experimental Self shows up in my conceptual thinking. A smaller part, for me, is the Rational Self, which shows up mostly in my logical thinking.

As is often the case for parents and children, my daughter's thinking preferences are similar to mine; we share high preferences in a couple of the thinking style quadrants. And, we are quite different as we tend to apply our thinking styles in a different order. An example is when we work together in the kitchen, baking. I first use my Safekeeping thinking by sticking closely to the recipe and following instructions step by step. In contrast, my daughter calls first on her Experimental thinking preferences and is not nearly as constrained by the specifics of the recipe. She is quite comfortable bringing her creative capabilities to the moment. Neither approach is right or wrong. They are simply different.

It's also possible for the thinking preferences of a parent and child to be quite different, even opposite. And, inside of a family, all the members may be very similar with the exception of one member who may seem totally different.

Do you have a *black sheep* in your family?

We did in mine. My brother, Steve, marched to his own drummer, and the relationship he had with our father was often difficult because Steve did not think and approach things like the rest of us. I think now that a lot of pain and suffering could have been avoided if there had been an opportunity for my father to see Steve's thinking preferences as different, but acceptable.

How Does Understanding Thinking Styles Improve Connection?

Our particular thinking styles strongly influence our actions, including the manner in which we speak and act, as well as how we perceive the actions of others and how we hear what they say. The greater the differences in the preferred thinking styles of two people, the greater the chance that there will be a disconnect in their communications.

Discovering the differences in our own style and the style of our adopted child allows us the opportunity to understand, rather than wonder why our child seems to be stubborn about thinking and acting in their own way. Our tendency is to think that if our child is processing things differently than we do, there's something wrong.

Instead, we as parents can develop the ability to see that our child's way of thinking and acting is, in fact, also right. There is no right or wrong in the different styles of thinking. We simply have differences.

Let's return to the example of how my daughter and I enjoy baking together. When I asked—or worse yet—when I *insisted* my daughter, who has the Experimental thinking style and likes to keep the big picture in mind, do something my way, based on my preferences, it was not helpful to her or our level of connection.

In the past when baking, I would instruct her to read the first step.

She would read it and then look at me and say, "Now what?"

To me, reading the step should have been enough. But, in her mind, as an Experimental thinker, she operates better when she has the whole story or the vision in mind, not just the first step.

She likes to understand: *Why?*

And, I was asking her to understand: *How?*

I didn't do it to frustrate her. I did it because that's *my* comfort zone. I did it because it came naturally to me. Once I understood our differences, I learned that we make more progress when we start by first thinking about what we are going to make; and then move to the ingredients and actions necessary to create those wonderful cookies or cakes that we're picturing. That process works better for her. She also brings that creative, experimental thinking preference to the activity. This can result in some new and tasty concoctions that would never exist if we always stuck with the recipe. We can enjoy the fun of baking without our preferences interfering with understanding each other.

A delightful outcome of our better understanding of each other's thinking preferences is that now we can joke with each other about our differences, rather than being frustrated by them.

FEELINGS AND NEEDS

At the very heart of connecting with our adopted child in a supportive and emotionally safe manner is our ability as parents to decipher their disruptive behaviors and get to the feelings and needs behind the behaviors.

As parents, one of the most important things we can do to help our adopted child is to assist them in getting their needs met. Even if a child is no longer an infant, we may need to help them shore up the foundation of their brain architecture so that they can catch up with age-appropriate emotional maturity. With emotional maturity comes the added bonus of the ability to feel safe, and therefore the ability to risk vulnerability, which in turn allows for the ability to trust and to give and receive love.

The Importance of Feelings

The feelings or emotions displayed by our children through their disruptive actions and through their unpleasant statements can be thought of as indicators of unmet needs.

My friend, Bill Stierle, of Corporate Culture Development, who is a recognized expert in interpersonal communications, says, "No one says or does anything unless a *need* of theirs is being met in the moment."

The instant I first heard him say this was another pivotal moment for me in my journey as an adoptive parent. My understanding was suddenly much clearer. When we think of behavior from the perspective of meeting needs, the feelings our child displays through their behaviors can literally become a treasure map to understanding that child.

Bill says, "Feelings are like the instrument gauges on the dashboard of our car. They give us an indication that something is wrong and needs our attention."

This is useful to us as parents because it helps us move from being puzzled about why our children are doing what they are doing to understanding that there is a purpose behind their behaviors. Our children don't understand what is going on inside them when they act out with negative feelings.

Our children don't decide: *I will do this specific behavior because I feel a certain way and because I have an unmet need.*

When they act out, however, children give us clues. Their brains use disruptive behaviors to meet an underlying need. When we know this, we also know to look behind the disruptive behavior for the need on which we should actually focus our attention.

When disruptive behaviors occur, we should imagine our child saying to us: *Mom, Dad, I need your help!*

Or, we can recognize their underlying plea as: *Please help me understand my pain!*

The Power of Unmet Needs

As human beings, we have a whole range of needs:

- *Foundational needs* are the physical ones, such as the needs related to survival, like our need for food, water, and air.

- *Reliability needs* are learning, play, and self-worth.

- *Independence needs* are kindness, closeness, family, and passion.

Over the first seventeen years of our lives, we build our emotional maturity one building block—or one emotional need—at a time. When a baby is separated from its biological mother, and when other traumas, such as physical or emotional neglect and abuse, occur in the life of a child, the establishment of the emotional foundation gets disrupted.

Emotional building blocks that are often weak or absent in adopted children include:

- Nurturance
- Bonding

- Comfort
- Love
- Touch
- Affection
- Acceptance

If these emotional building blocks aren't present in the life of a child between birth and two years old, it makes it very difficult for them to develop other needs at the appropriate age including:

- Choice
- Stability
- Trust
- Fairness
- Understanding
- Friendship

By the age of seventeen, children who have not had their needs met will likely be missing or unsure of qualities, such as:

- Independence
- Respect
- Integrity
- Recognition

It can be confusing for us as our adopted children grow, or if we adopt an older child, let's say a tween or teenager, because they are in physical bodies that are reflective of their age. In fact, research suggests that they may even be ahead in their physical development. So, because they look a certain age, we are inclined to have an expectation that their emotional development is as advanced as their physical development. Much of the time this is not true. They often lag several years behind in emotional development. I know many parents who have marveled that their adopted teenager seems to act like a five-year-old, but it's probably not a coincidence. He's not doing it on purpose. He's just got a foundation that needs to be shored up.

Compassionate Communication

Nonviolent Communication, or alternatively, *Compassionate Communication,* the communication technique created by Marshall B. Rosenberg, has been used for more than fifty years across the globe to reduce conflict and allow for peaceful connection in highly volatile situations.

As I introduce this technique to clients, I refer to it as *Compassionate Communication.*

Compassionate Communication addresses the issues of feelings and needs.

The technique has four basic steps:

1. **Observe the behavior or statement** without interpretation or judgment; it is an observation of *exactly* what happened or was said.

2. **Identify a feeling or feelings;** this requires some curiosity because we can't ever know exactly what another person is feeling; we can only *guess* what they may be feeling and ask for confirmation about our accuracy.

3. **Identify a need or needs;** this also requires curiosity. Based on the circumstances that we are confronted with, we can usually make some pretty good guesses to gain clarity.

4. **Make a clear and present request** of the other person.

Putting it all together might sound something like this: "When you said, 'No', could it be that you were feeling frustrated about my telling you to get ready for dinner because you have a need for a choice right now about whether or not to stop playing your video game?"

The child might answer: "Yeah," and then we would proceed to a request.

Or they might say: "No."

Then, we make another guess at a feeling and a need because again, we can't know without asking and getting confirmation. Bringing curiosity to that moment will allow us to discover the feeling and need.

Once we have clarified and established their need, we can make a request that will address both our needs:

- *Our need* for the health of our child through nourishment
- *Our child's need* for choice in that moment

I want to be very clear that this is not about just letting a child have their own way. It is about getting needs met: the needs of both the parent *and* the child, because after all, we both have needs.

I purposefully used the example above of a child's *need for choice*. This need is often unmet and very alive in an adopted child. We can easily see that they might have a belief that they have no choice in their lives. Whether that is factually true or not is not the immediate issue.

Adopted children have often experienced:

- Separation from their biological family
- Placement in institutional care
- Moving around in the foster care system
- Chosen by others to be adopted
- Leaving familiar surroundings in order to live somewhere else
- Separation from their country of birth and cultural heritage
- Losing their original language

They didn't choose any of these experiences. *Choice* can be a huge unmet need for these children. Finding a way to allow them to have a choice in even the smallest of matters within their new home and family is essential, and will greatly benefit your attempts to establish trust.

EMPATHY

One of the most powerful ways that we can connect as human beings is through the act of giving *empathy* to each other. Empathizing is one of the most healing interaction skills that we can have. The act of empathizing alone can provide our child with a space in which they can be really seen, heard and known; perhaps for the very first time in their lives.

Empathy Versus Sympathy

Empathy is different from *sympathy*. Sympathy is a wonderful feeling and has an appropriate use. Sympathizing is more like putting yourself in somebody else's shoes. It is only part of the way to demonstrate care and understanding.

Sympathizing might sound something like this:

- *I understand how you are feeling.*
- *I see you're feeling sad.*
- *It's alright.*
- *It'll be okay.*
- *I've experienced what you are experiencing because I also went through the same thing that you've gone through.*

These are beautiful, caring sentences, but they are not providing empathy.

In the webinars Bill Stierle and I teach, he says, "Empathy only occurs when *feeling* words and *need* words are connected with each other, and agreed on by the participants in the conversation."

Empathy is at the heart of the four-step Compassionate Communication technique mentioned earlier. Let's return to my example of telling the child it is time to eat.

An empathetic question might sound like this: *Could you be feeling angry because your need for choice was not met just now?*

When this or another curious and empathetic guess resonates with the child, they will respond affirmatively. At that point, you can make a request that addresses both your needs and the child's needs that are alive in that present moment.

It might sound like this: *Would you be willing to finish what you're doing within the next five minutes and come to the table?*

At first, these empathetic interactions may require a bit of back and forth; or they may be met with resistance by the child. Nonetheless, with consistent use of the Compassionate Communication approach, the *magic* will occur.

For instance, the child might say *yes* or might say: *I want to have ten more minutes.*

In either case, the child has had an opportunity for choice, and they will in all likelihood come to the table without further resistance at that time.

Why?

The child will connect because their feelings and needs are being acknowledged and valued.

Remember, your need in that moment—your need for your child to get nourishment by eating—has also been met. A bonus set of your needs can be met, too, including your needs for cooperation and peace.

Nonetheless, I have had more than one client that has said something like: *But, I want him to come to the table the first time I tell him to! I'm not here to negotiate with a kid.*

When we feel this way, we need to keep our goal of a connected relationship with our child in mind. We can certainly take the tack of insisting on immediate obedience. I did for a long time with my daughter. But, it never resulted in the connection that I desired. I had to change my approach.

In order to change my approach, though, I had to learn to start with self-empathy.

Self-Empathy

When we want to help our children, we need to make sure that we are coming from a place that feels safe for ourselves because it is easy to be triggered in situations with them. Sometimes, what our children do and say can trigger us into reactions that may not be helpful to having the presence and connection that we want and need to have. Therefore, one of the steps in having a connected interaction with our child is to check-in with ourselves first. We must realize if we are being triggered or having some reaction to what is being said or done.

There have been times in my journey with my daughter when I felt like I was continuously triggered by her actions. It's not unusual for a parent to have a child do something that's insulting, rude, or disobedient, and for us to have a triggered reaction that this child is not providing us with respect.

We can help ourselves and our relationship tremendously at that moment by developing the skill of checking-in with ourselves when we observe the behavior and having a self-dialogue similar to the following:

- *What are my own needs in this moment?*
- *What self-empathy do I need to give to myself right now?*
- *The thing this child just said or did does not meet my need for respect.*
- *Okay, now I know what I am feeling because I've given myself self-empathy.*

I am now in a better position to not let that need push me into a reaction that is not going to be helpful in this situation.

With practice, our ability to pause in the moment and have this type of inner dialogue becomes easier. Will we always be able to do it this way? No. I can't always do it; but I can now do it most of the time.

Even the creator of the Nonviolent Communication Process, Marshall B. Rosenberg, PhD, is reported by colleagues to have said that he failed in his responses multiple times each day. So, we can all relieve ourselves of unrealistic expectations of perfection. As we practice Compassionate Communication, some, and then many, and then most of our interactions with our child will become more peaceful. The children will become more connected. They will become calmer.

Holding Space for the Child

There is something magical that happens when we can be fully present for another person who is in distress. This can be true about interactions with our children if we can observe their behaviors in a nonjudgmental way and simply see what's going on. We can check in with ourselves with self-empathy to make sure that we are aware of our needs that may be triggered in that moment.

If we can pause and take a breath and bring our attention to our child with curiosity, we can experience gratitude that we have the knowledge and understanding that the behaviors our child is displaying—and the emotion that comes with those behaviors—are clues for us. Then, we are in a position to hold the space for that child.

We can help our child by doing the following:

- Demonstrate calmness and presence.
- Help them understand their own feelings.
- Be strong and curious for and with them.

In many ways, we can make it a sacred space:

- Imagine a bubble around ourselves and our child in that moment.

- Bring an intention and a desire to be present for them.

- Find out what their need is and what we are going to be able to do to help them get their need met in that moment.

- Help them recognize their needs to the extent that they are able at their age.

- Collaborate with them to find a resolution for that moment that is safe and life-affirming for them and for us.

CHAPTER FIVE

A Peaceful Home Is Possible

SAFETY, TRUST, AND CONNECTION

Adoptive mother and author of *Love Lessons: Understanding, Learning, and Finding Purpose While Raising Challenging Children*, Jodi Bean, writes in her blog that her adopted daughter "lied about *everything*" when she first arrived home. "It was a bit crazy. And now I see, it was simply a huge billboard hanging from her neck that said: *I don't trust you, I don't feel safe.*" (findinghopefoundation.com, July 24, 2012)

The moment we understand the possibility and truth of this for our adopted child, we will quickly get to a place where we can help them in a truly meaningful way. The work of establishing a meaningful connection with our adopted child is probably the most important responsibility that we have as adoptive parents.

Our adopted child's connection with us provides the platform for them to have other meaningful and connected relationships in their lives. It requires us to not just provide an environment that is safe, but to interact with them in ways that create emotional safety for them. The connection and trust between adopted children and their parents provides them the opportunity to let go of hypervigilance, to create a space in which they can risk being vulnerable, and thereby, learn to trust.

Safety

My adopted daughter has the fantastic gift of being able to put a lot of what she feels into writing. On one occasion, she wrote a long description of the feeling of anxiety that is her constant companion. Like her, many children with early trauma may appear to be calm but their brains are on high alert, constantly scanning their environment, vigilant to every word, sound, movement, glance, and action around them to see if it holds some form of danger for them.

As the parents of anxious children, we need to be ready to observe and communicate with their state of anxiety much of the time. They often have a core belief that the world is not safe and that adult caregivers will not protect them from harm. This comes from their past experiences. Adopted children also have an unconscious expectation that we as parents should know that they are in pain.

Sometimes, we must do the work of setting aside our own expectations and beliefs about appropriate behavior. We must stop explaining and lecturing about the consequences of what our children choose to do.

Except when we must intervene with protective force to prevent serious harm to themselves or others, sometimes we must simply accept when they've done a hard, hard thing that we don't like or of which we don't approve.

Sometimes, we must allow for the possibility of our own personal embarrassment to prove to our children that what they choose to do to test our willingness to stick with them and accept them will not destroy our love for them and will not drive us away.

I hope you are never faced with this because it can be extremely hard. It may test every fiber of your being.

Trust

In order to truly have a connected relationship with another person that is mutually satisfactory and meets our needs for reciprocity, trust must exist in that relationship. Trust does not exist in the absence of vulnerability. And vulnerability—the exposure of oneself to the possibility of being physically or emotionally injured—is extremely difficult, even impossible if the person does not feel safe.

A major objective of the parent of a traumatized child must be the creation of opportunities for the child to be vulnerable, to take a chance, to risk revealing their feelings.

How do we do this?

Trust has a lot to do with support. The practice of checking in with our child to see where support is needed, and then providing that support, allows for trust to develop. This helps the child find out that there is a safe place in which they can risk being more vulnerable. This can require a lot of time, attention, and support.

The good news is that we don't need large, carefully constructed activities to allow trust to be developed. We don't have to wait for big, dramatic, emotional events to come along that we survive together. Rather, trust is developed in the small, day-after-day moments of support, choice, acceptance, emotional safety, and consideration. Our adopted children need the times that we as parents are present for them—over and over again.

There is healing in frequently and repeatedly affirming devotion out loud.

There is healing in the small, loving things we say and do, even during the roughest moments.

We can remember and honor:

- Their preferences, such as their favorite color, food, ice cream, toy, story, game
- The way they like their sandwich cut
- The name of their best friend at school

And we can express our affection and gratitude, saying things like:

- *"I love you."*
- *"I'm glad you are my daughter."*
- *"God gave me the best gift ever when He brought you to me."*
- *"I am the luckiest Mom in the world."*
- *"No matter what you do, I will always love you."*

Additionally, there are actions we can take:

- Let them have choices, and then support those choices, even if they are not what we would have preferred.

- Ask them how they feel, listening to the reply and letting it be, without suggesting that they should not feel that way.

- Give them the freedom and choice to ask for our help. Let them know we are there to provide support if needed, rather than automatically jumping in to fix every problem they have.

These are the little things that lead to trust.

Connection

At a very difficult moment in my daughter's life, she felt overwhelmed, frustrated, victimized, and misunderstood.

She sent an email to me that said:

> *I do not trust you. I don't care if you are disappointed in me because everyone is always disappointed with me. Nobody really cares about me. Everyone just lies. You don't love me, you are just sick of dealing with me. Why don't you just send me back?*

There, in black and white, was the ultimate question.

It can be phrased in countless ways:

- *Why don't you stop trying?*
- *Why don't you just give up on me?*
- *Can't you see I'm hopeless? Worthless? Not worth your time and effort?*
- *Why don't you hate me the way I hate myself?*

Clearly, she was in a great deal of pain and needed connection but felt that she wasn't connected with anyone, including me. All she could do was speak about the pain that she felt in the best way that she could.

My response was short and simple. You may recognize it as the dedication statement at the beginning of this book.

I replied, "I loved you yesterday, I love you today, and I will love you tomorrow."

I meant every word.

I know you feel the same way about your child.

As humans, we are meant to live in relationships. What we seek as parents is congruency between the harmonious relationship we desire and our daily interactions with our child.

As adoptive parents, we must:

- Assure that the language we use does not unintentionally increase conflict

- Evaluate the congruency between our beliefs about parenting and our goals for internal calm within our homes

- Examine our strategies for discipline to insure they do not work against, rather than for, true connection

- Assure that our own thinking and communication preferences do not block us from communicating and interacting in ways that allow us to hear and be heard in ways that meet our objective of harmony

LIMITS

It is important for all people to have some limits and boundaries in their lives. It provides us with safety and stability. Developing self-control and an ability to self-regulate is essential for a child to develop as part of their emotional maturity. For a traumatized child, we must help them to develop these skills because other thoughts and feelings that are operating in their minds—and the coping skills that their brains use—often work against their having appropriate personal limits.

Tolerating Frustration

Something that is difficult for a child who has been traumatized to learn is how to tolerate frustrating circumstances. Because of the high anxiety and hypervigilance that often goes along with anxiety, as well as the need for control and safety, it can be very difficult for an anxious child to be in a situation where they feel threatened or unsafe and they are unable to manifest control.

We need to provide situations where our child can practice feeling frustrated in a safe way. This needs to be introduced gradually to them so they can build up the emotional muscle needed to be resilient in situations where their normal response may be to overreact. This practice is important because many situations in life, as we all know, can be very frustrating and are often beyond our control. Our child may exhibit their frustration or anger in inappropriate and even destructive ways. So, learning to respect boundaries, tolerate frustration, and stay within reasonable limits of behavior are essential and require practice.

Delaying Gratification

Another essential skill for human beings is to be able to understand and practice the ability to not always require immediate gratification for everything that we want. Much like tolerating frustration, delaying gratification prepares a child to be resilient in real situations that they will be faced with throughout their lives.

Sometimes, immediate gratification is a way of feeling secure, and it may even be a way of fulfilling a need for belonging. Immediate gratification may also be a way for a child to feel like they are in control of their world. Children need to be able to tolerate the fact that the world is not always going to give them everything they want exactly when they want it.

In order to be able to participate in many activities of life, children need the ability to delay gratification in order to:

- Interact with other people
- Share space with other people
- Form relationships

Developing Impulse Control

Sometimes, children who have been traumatized have such high anxiety that when they become focused on an idea or thought, they feel a compulsion to act on that thought immediately. They may not be able to keep themselves from saying something they're feeling out loud, even if it is socially inappropriate to say.

Traumatized children also might not be able to hold themselves back from speaking out loud in a situation where they are not supposed to speak without permission. This can be common in school when they know an answer or hear an answer given by another child that they believe is incorrect. They may not be able to hold themselves back from speaking out and correcting their classmate.

A client of mine told me about a circumstance in which her daughter was in class, and a classmate wrote something on the blackboard. Her daughter saw the answer was partially incorrect. She could not restrain herself from getting up from her desk and going to the board to correct the other girl's work. Then, she felt embarrassed, and when she sat back down, she did not have the self-control to keep from laughing out loud.

The client's daughter was nervously laughing at herself. But, the impression that she made on others was that she was laughing at the girl whose work she had corrected. This caused a misunderstanding, and she was reprimanded by the teacher and embarrassed in front of her classmates. The ability to control her impulses was a necessary skill for her to learn, and it took time.

LIVING IN GRATITUDE

I think that having and expressing gratitude is one of the most beneficial actions we can practice as adoptive parents.

I like a quote I read in a daily calendar from American motivational speaker, businessman, and author Tony Robbins: "When you are grateful, fear disappears and abundance appears."

Today, I feel so much gratitude for my adopted daughter, Emilia. I feel gratitude for the lessons learned that helped me understand who she is, what she feels, and what her struggles are. I feel so much gratitude for the individuals who have helped me learn how to help her best. I have extreme gratitude for everyone who has read this book. I am grateful for your love for your own adopted child, and for your journey to a harmonious and connected life with your child.

The Power of Gratitude

Gratitude is powerful because it invites and requires us to step away from thoughts that are negative. Gratitude gives us the opportunity to pause and bring to mind the good in our lives that is sometimes overshadowed by the business of daily life.

As adoptive parents, it is especially powerful and useful to remember with gratitude that we have been given the opportunity to influence the life of a child who otherwise may not have had the opportunity to live in a family. Without adoption, our child might not have grown up with connected relationships that provide belonging, safety, and stability where they could flourish. Gratitude is a gift that we give ourselves when we otherwise might feel that so much in our lives is negative.

Naming Something You're Grateful for Each Day

A helpful practice can be having a time or a place each day in our lives when we pause and name something we are grateful for. We all can be grateful for many things each day.

I have a podcast, *Adopted: Now What?* In each session, I start and end with a statement of gratitude. Sometimes, my gratitude is for something that is very emotional or extremely meaningful to me. I almost always have tears in my eyes when I mention the gratitude that I have for various aspects of my life with my daughter. And, sometimes my statements of gratitude are for simple everyday things in my life. Sometimes, they are that both the microphone and our computer system are working at the same time.

The magic comes in stepping away from the daily activities that we are all so busy with, and taking a moment—even if it is just in your mind—and feeling gratitude. Begin by naming what is in your heart that you are thankful for in the moment. An even more powerful thing to do is write your statements of gratitude. You could put them into a journal, or on a notepad and post them on top of your computer, mirror, or wherever it is that you can see them during the hours of the day when you're going about your normal activities.

Helping Our Children Find the Magic of Gratitude

Because our adopted children have experienced trauma and feel so much anxiety and because they have sometimes abandoned their natural childlike state in order to focus on being in control and protecting themselves, it is especially important that we help them learn how to recognize things for which they can feel gratitude. We need to help our children see and name those things.

With a very small child, recognizing gratitude can be as simple as asking them which toy they like, or maybe even which crayon they are happy is in the box. Gratitude can begin with something that simple. Getting in a habit of speaking as parents about what we are grateful for and encouraging our child to find and be able to express what they are grateful for is essential and healing. It is essential because there are plenty of alarming thoughts going on in their head. And, helping our child move into a place of identifying what is positive and what they are happy exists in their lives—no matter how small—is very important.

Conclusion

I cannot imagine a greater calling or a more noble action than for one human being to open up their heart and home to another human being that needs a place to belong and thrive. This is what you have done as an adoptive parent, or what you are considering doing as a prospective adoptive parent. I am so grateful for you. It is a huge journey. It changes our lives just like any addition to our family changes our lives. And, like many adventures, we go into it with great enthusiasm and anticipation about the success, happiness, fun, and joy that we are going to experience.

During the adoption process, we may imagine how happy our adopted child is going to feel that we saved them, that we took them out of a situation sometimes filled with neglect, violence, and abuse. We bring them into a safe, peaceful, and attentive environment in which they can belong as our children. Sometimes, there are unpleasant surprises on that journey, but that does not make the journey any less valuable.

We can help our child if we can understand what some of those surprises really mean. And, we can be prepared to evaluate our own thoughts and feelings about what is happening and to make sure they don't take us down a path that is unhelpful. We can recognize the behaviors, statements, and actions of our adopted children for what they truly are: they are coping mechanisms that their brains have created to help them feel safe in the world in which they have been living.

With presence and patience, it's possible to bring our children out of a mode of operation where they rely on unhealthy coping skills. This happens through our love and underlying desires to give them the environment that we want them to have—one that is peaceful, where they feel safe, and believe that they belong. We want our children to have a home that allows them to be themselves even when there are upsets. There will be ups and downs, but they and we can have the connection and the resilience that will allow us to return as quickly as possible to a place of harmony.

If there is one *most important thing* that I can encourage you to do as an adoptive parent, it is to give yourself a break.

What does this mean?

It means understanding that you are doing the best you can do with what you have at the moment. There are ways to improve the skills and strategies that we have so that we may change the outcome of our interactions with our adopted children. But, we can't change until we understand what those strategies are and have practiced them enough to be comfortable with them. Then, we can utilize the strategies in the moments when there is distress, upset, or conflict. Those moments occur in *all* families.

I encourage you—when there is a statement or an action by your adopted child that is disruptive, or feels like less than you would want it to be—I encourage you to:

- Observe without judgment.
- Strip away interpretations and simply see the action.
- Hear their statements without judgment.

I want you to check in with yourself and feel what you're feeling, and find out what need is alive in you in the moment.

Ask yourself:

- *Do I need peace?*
- *Do I need rest?*
- *Do I need cooperation?*

Then, I want you to think about the feeling your child is displaying and what need they might have behind their statement.

If they are angry, is it because they have a need for clarity?

If they are frustrated, is it because they have a need for choice in the moment?

Once you have identified both your own feelings and needs and those of your child, make a request of yourself or of your child. Make a request that includes an opportunity for you *both* to have what you need at the moment. Remember, this is not about letting our children simply have their own way. This is not about not ever having them do what we want or need them to do. This is about being aware of both their needs and our needs because it's an understanding of those needs that provides the opportunity for connection. It provides the opportunity for truly seeing and understanding each other.

I love the fact that I have not yet coached an adoptive parent who has not turned out to be the right parent for their adopted child.

As adoptive parents, we can feel we are the right parent if we allow ourselves to do so—even when we are tired, frustrated, and it seems that everything we have tried to do has not worked.

The right parent is the parent who:

- Strives to understand what is going on inside their child

- Learns to see beyond the behavior to the reality of their child's needs

- Sees the needs their child has that were not fulfilled by the caregivers elsewhere in their life

- Seeks to understand the coping mechanisms that their child's brain has created to keep them feeling safe

- Is willing to stand back and observe

- Remembers to take care of themselves

- Has self-empathy when feeling hurt, sad, frustrated, irritated, overwhelmed, or angry

- Understands the past trauma of their adopted child is healed one present moment at a time

I became the right parent for my adopted daughter.

I believe you can be the right parent for your adopted child, too.

Next Steps

As adoptive parents, we are in a position, day-by-day, one moment at a time, to provide our adopted children the best chance at overcoming the impact of the traumas that they have experienced. It takes time. It takes diligent effort. It takes external support. Beyond Adoptions exists to help you on your journey as an adoptive parent.

Visit our website: BeyondAdoptions.com. You are welcome to sign-up for a complimentary coaching session so we can:

- Hear you story
- Provide empathy for what you are experiencing
- Help you identify your parenting goals
- Establish a plan for achieving those goals

Beyond Adoptions coaching and support groups are primarily provided via teleconferencing, so you can benefit from the convenience of not having to be in a particular location to receive our services.

Tune in to my podcast: *Adopted: Now What?;* which is devoted to the voices of adoptive parents and adoptees. We share stories and information to help each other on our individual and unique journeys to self-fulfillment and the establishment of the compassionate, connected relationships we desire. Become part of our dedicated listening community. Share your experiences with other adoptive parents who know what you're talking about.

Like us on Facebook at BeyondAdoptions for information about our webinars, live training sessions, and information on compassionate parenting.

We look forward to hearing your story and supporting your journey!

About the Author

Becky Walker is an adoptive mother, personal coach, podcaster, blogger, and public speaker. Over eleven years ago, Becky adopted a little girl from Russia. Their relationship was a mess from the moment they walked out of the orphanage. Becky was inexperienced but determined to fix things between them. She sought help from professionals in the adoption industry, therapists, ministers, and friends but continued to struggle. Eventually, after a lot of trial and error, and with a deep desire to create a loving and peaceful connection, Becky finally discovered the strategies that would provide them with the connected relationship for which she had long wished.

After a thirty-seven-year career in the pharmaceutical and medical device industry, Becky knew down deep what she wanted to do next: to become a life coach and help other adoptive parents. Becky's research revealed that many adoptive parents still did not have ready access to the support and information that could help them create peaceful and connected relationships with their adopted children.

Therefore, with the full support of her daughter for the idea, that out of their own painful experience, an opportunity to help others was available. Becky decided to focus her coaching practice in the post-adoption area. She founded Beyond Adoptions, where Parent-to-Parent™ coaching services, online support groups, webinars, podcasts, blogs, and live training programs provide the perfect opportunities to share the different strategies and Compassionate Communication techniques to reduce conflict and provide the connection that can help address the unmet needs of adopted children. Becky is dedicated to giving value and easing the path for other adoptive parents by providing empathetic support, encouragement, and practical, effective strategies that can be applied every day within the home.

To find out more: BeyondAdoptions.com; (817) 888-0760; Becky@BeyondAdoptions.com

www.ingramcontent.com/pod-product-compliance
Lightning Source LLC
Chambersburg PA
CBHW070016110426
42741CB00034B/1997